The

ABCs

of

Biochemistry

By

Margot Alesund

 is for amino acids,

the building blocks of proteins,

the sequence to combine them

is encoded in our genes.

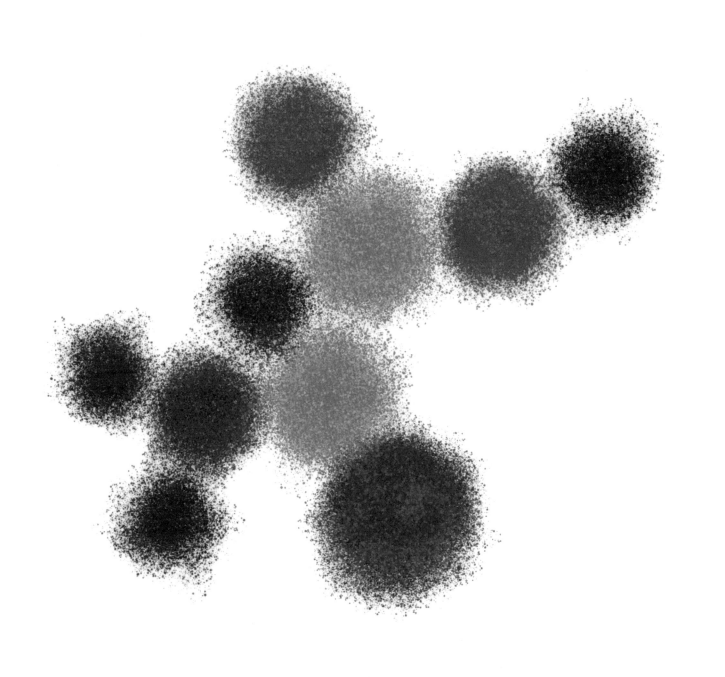

 is for buffer,

they keep the pH of solutions stable.

Without them, most our experiments wouldn't work.

We'd be unable.

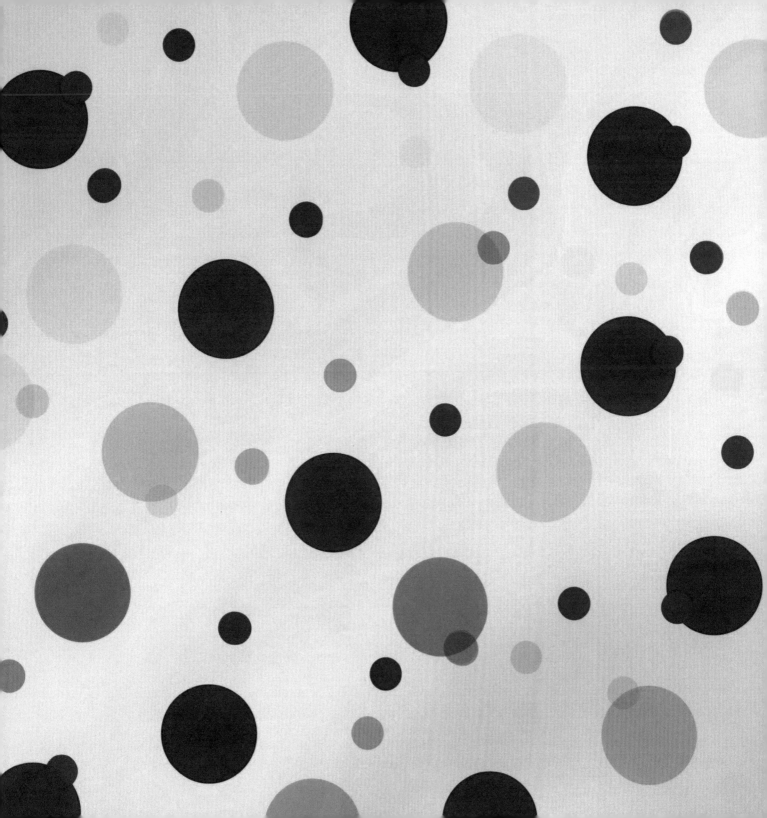

 is for confocal microscope,

it lets us see beautiful images of cells.

We can add labels and dyes,

to light up creatures, proteins, and organelles.

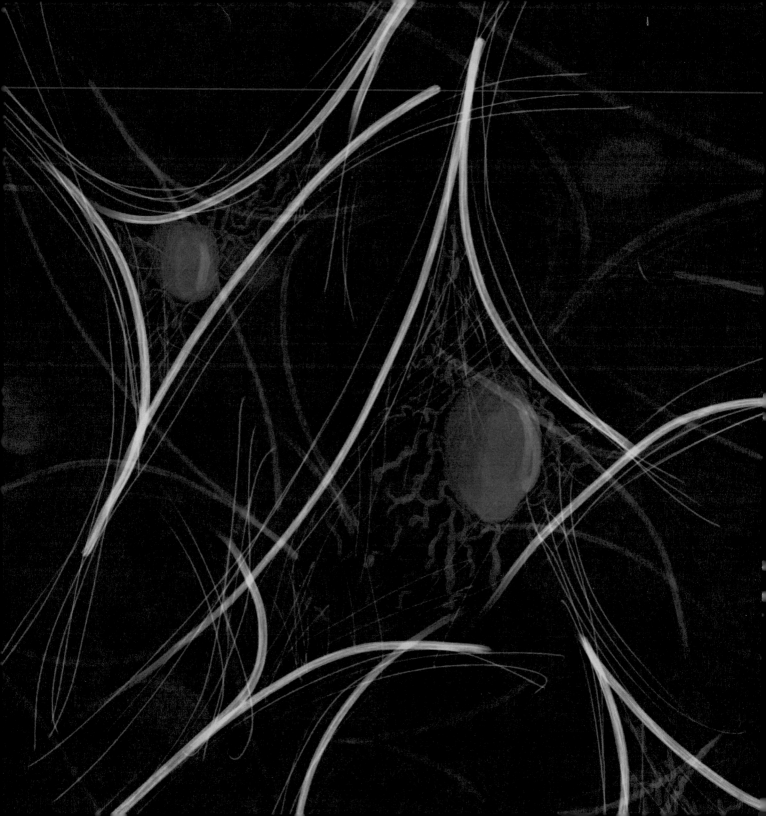

 is for DNA,

the instructions that our cells read,

Every lifeform on our planet has it,

from humans to seaweed.

 is for enzymes,

they're proteins that make reactions faster.

One enzyme can only do one task,

but of that they are the master.

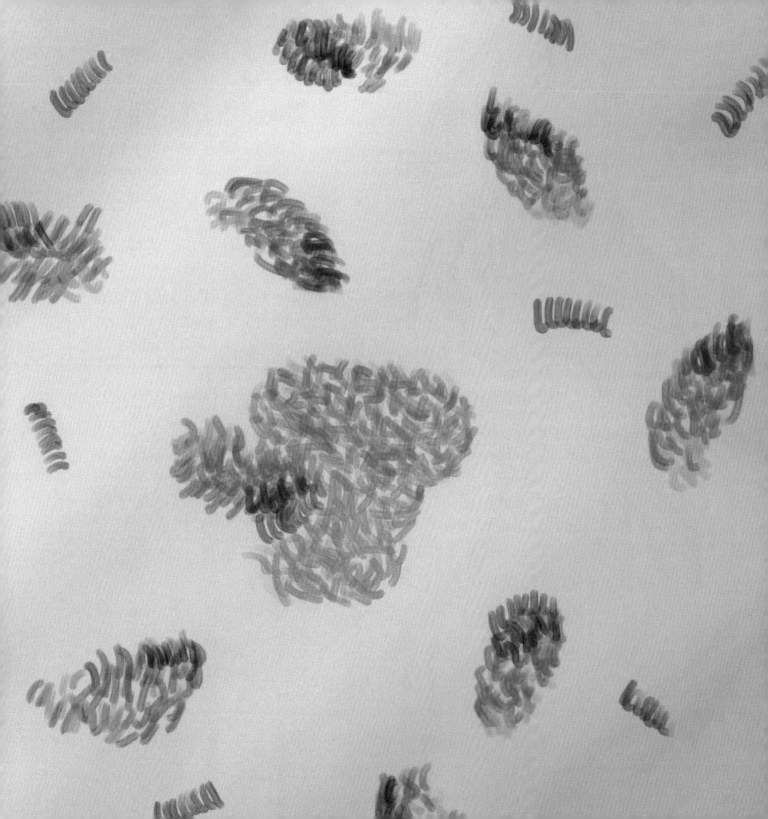

 is for fluorescent proteins,

they illuminate where proteins go.

We can genetically encode them,

so our protein of interest glows.

 is for gel electrophoresis,

it separates proteins or nucleic acids before our eyes.

An electrical field pulls the molecules through a porous gel,

smaller ones travel faster, separating by charge and size.

 is for hypothesis,

a guess that we frame

to guide experimental planning.

To support or disprove is the aim.

 is for isotopic labeling,

a technique that uses radiation

to track details of reactions,

especially an atom's molecular location.

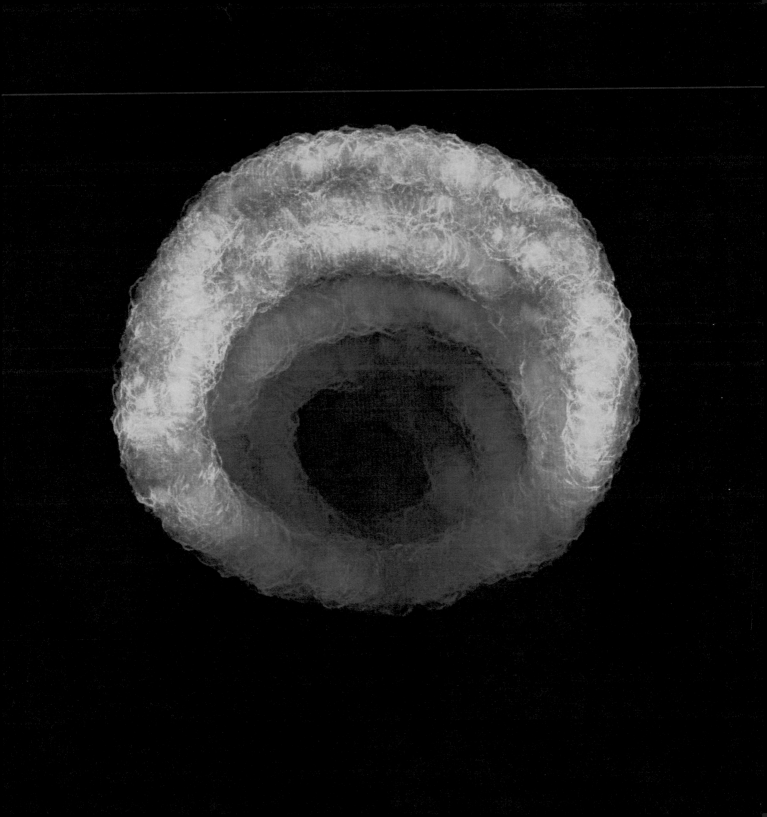

 is for journal,

the place where we declare

the discoveries we have made

so all the world's aware.

 is for kinetics,

the study of how fast reactions go.

Which enzyme is faster? Which drug works better?

This kinetics will show.

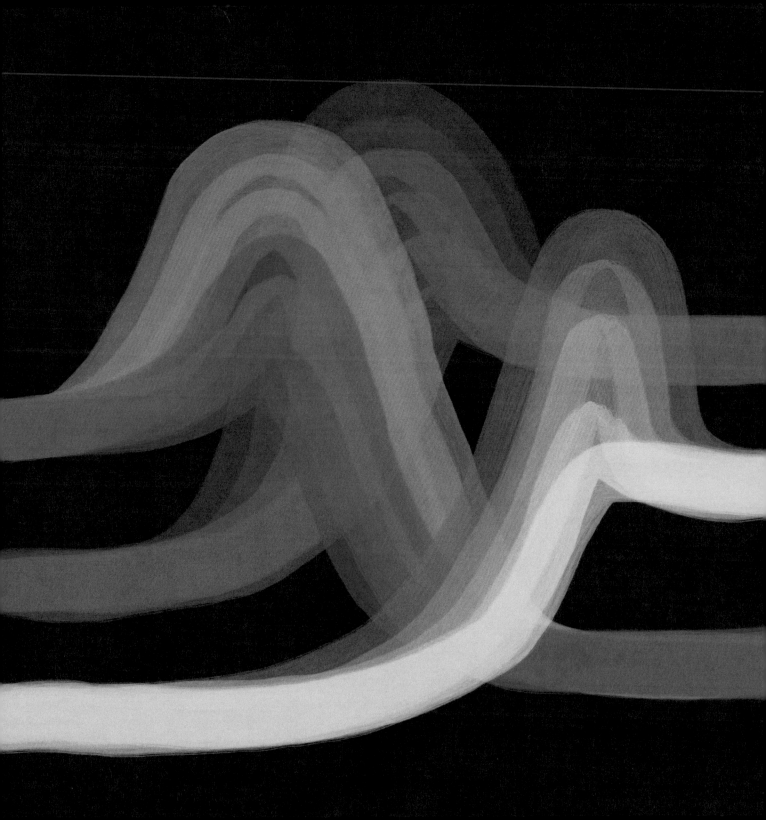

 is for lipids,

they have many roles.

Energy storage, cell communication, and membranes,

lots of jobs do they control.

 is for myosin,

one of the most amazing proteins you'll see!

It "walks" along actin

to move the muscles of you and me.

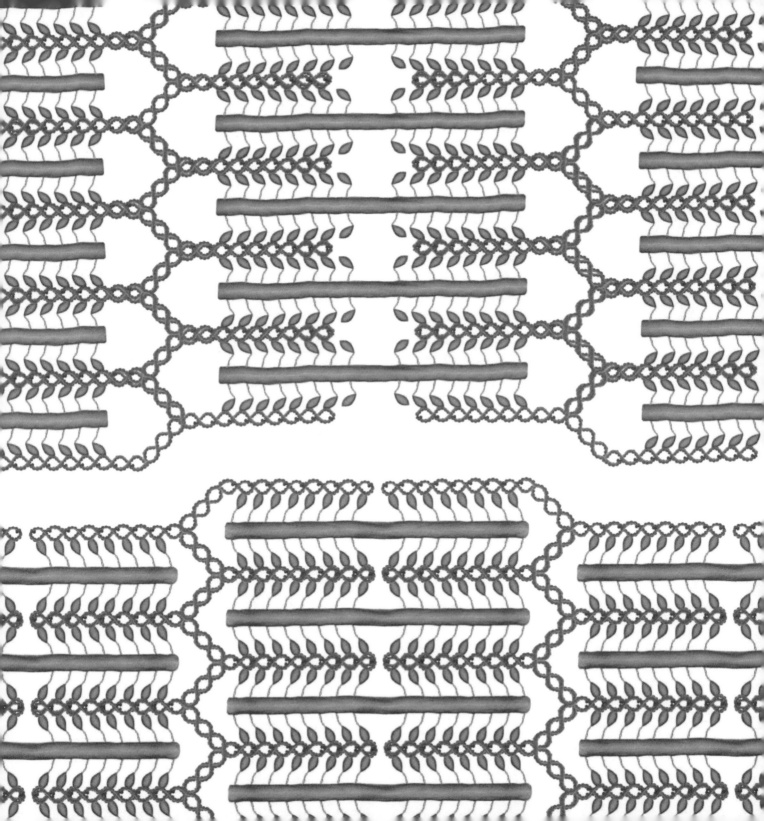

 is for notebook,

scientists have used them since way back when

to record our experiments

so we can repeat them over again.

June 8, 2016

Continued from pg 30

This PCR was to amplify Round 4 of the glycopeptide selection.

Master Mix

12.5 μl	10x PCR Buffer
2.5 μl	50 mM MgCl₂
2.5 μl	10 mM dNTP's
5 μl	10 μM forward primer
5 μl	10 μM reverse primer
5 μl	5ᵁ/μl hot start Taq
66.5 μl	dd H₂O
1 μl	¹/₁₀₀₀ SYBR Green

mix split into 5 tubes. 5 μl of RT mix of each trial added to a tube, 5 μl dd H₂O added to no template control

	1 min	94°C
x20 {	15 sec	94°C
	15 sec	65°C
	30 sec	72°C
	hold	4°C

* Real time graph on next page

 is for observation,

during an experiment we try to discern,

What happened? What changed? How does this work?

We observe, then record to learn.

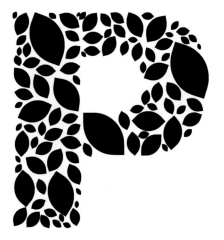 is for photoreceptor,

cells that permit sleep and sight.

They send a signal to your brain

when they absorb a certain type of light.

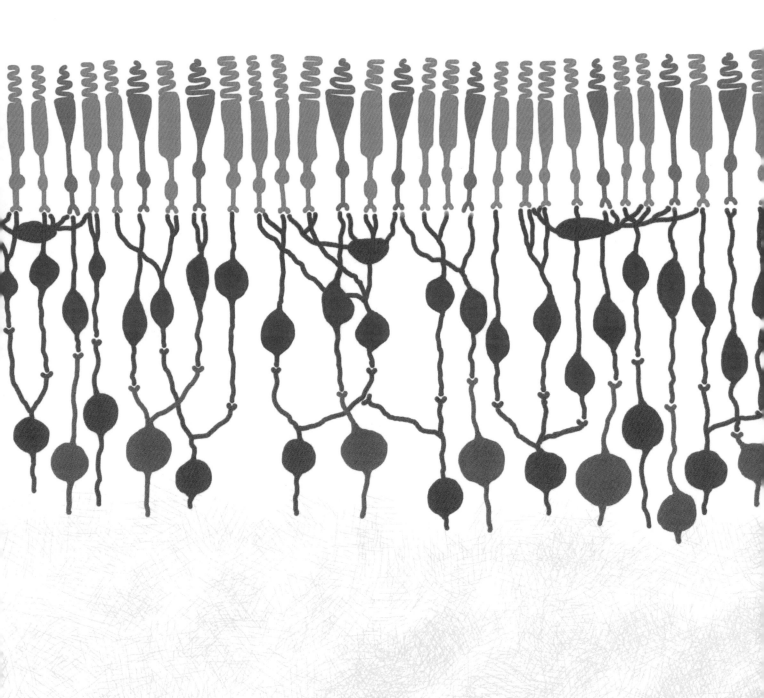

 is for qualitative analysis,

which helps us tell "What's in here?"

NMR, spectroscopy, and mass spectrometry

can make the answer more clear.

 is for RNA,

a biomolecule of many talents.

Once thought to only code for proteins,

also regulates our genes' expression balance.

 is for sequencing,

DNA sequencing to be exact.

It tells us the order of nucleotides

and, on science, has had great impact.

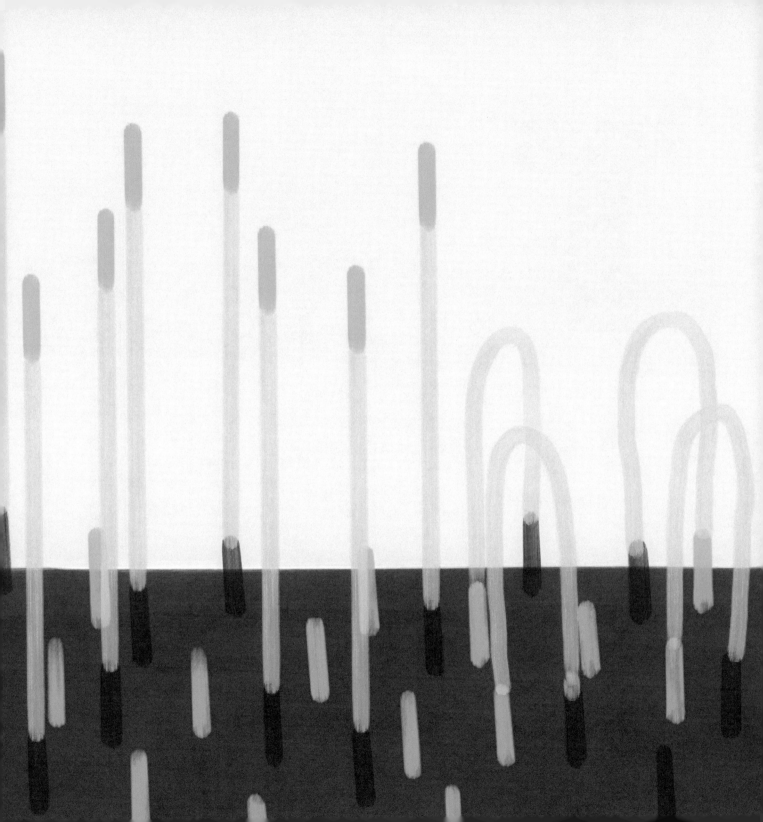

 is for Taq Polymerase,

the enzyme that inspired PCR.

Without it, biotech, medicine, and forensics

wouldn't have gotten so very far.

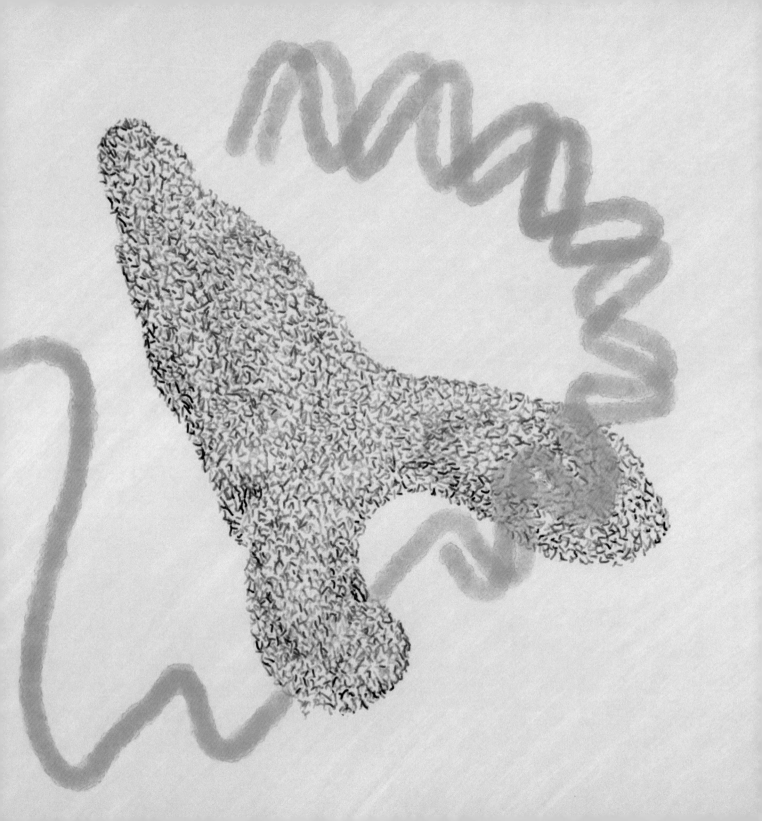

 is for ultracentrifugation,

a technique that spins a sample with great speed.

Size, shape, and interactions with other molecules

can be determined from this, indeed.

 is for vectors,

special types of DNA

used to introduce genes into an organism

to change them in a certain way.

 is for wavelength,

a measurement of light.

A fingerprint of a molecule

is the wavelengths they emit or excite.

 is for xenobiotics,

a term which simply refers to

a foreign substance in one's body.

They can hurt you or can serve you.

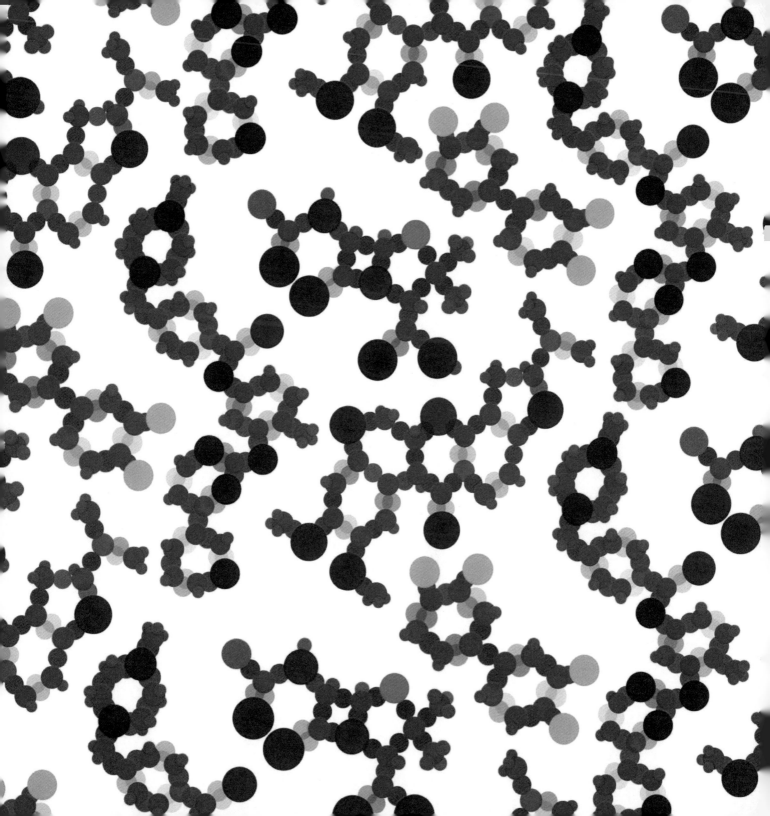

 is for yeast,

an incredibly well studied fungi.

Humans have similar biological pathways,

so research on yeast, to humans it may apply.

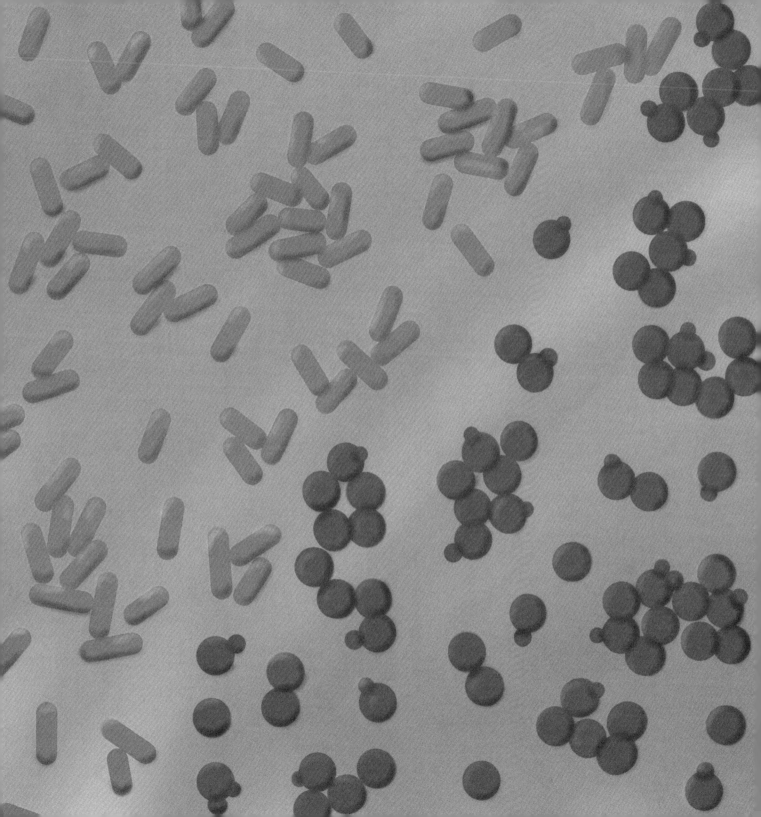

 is for zwitterion,

molecules that are quite useful.

They have a negative and positive charge

that cancel out to make them neutral.

Now we're all done!
You know your ABCs!
Maybe soon you can start
doing biochemistry!

A B C D E F

G H I J K L

M N O P Q

R S T U V

W X Y Z 🧪

Explore
THE BABY BIOCHEMIST
Series

The Baby Biochemist: DNA

The Baby Biochemist: RNA

The Baby Biochemist: Proteins

The Baby Biochemist: Enzymatics

@TheBabyBiochemist

@BabyBiochemist

Follow The Baby Biochemist on social media for new books, science projects, activities, and more!

Made in the USA
Middletown, DE
02 June 2017